25th International Conference on Computational Linguistics

(COLING 2014)

Tutorial Abstracts

Dublin, Ireland
23 - 29 August 2014

ISBN: 978-1-63439-197-9

Printed from e-media with permission by:

Curran Associates, Inc.
57 Morehouse Lane
Red Hook, NY 12571

Some format issues inherent in the e-media version may also appear in this print version.

Printed by Curran Associates, Inc. (2014)

For permission requests, please contact the Association for Computational Linguistics
at the address below.

Association for Computational Linguistics
209 N. Eighth Street
Stroudsburg, Pennsylvania 18360

Phone: 1-570-476-8006
Fax: 1-570-476-0860

acl@aclweb.org

Additional copies of this publication are available from:

Curran Associates, Inc.
57 Morehouse Lane
Red Hook, NY 12571 USA
Phone: 845-758-0400
Fax: 845-758-2634
Email: curran@proceedings.com
Web: www.proceedings.com

Preface

This volume contains papers from the 25th International Conference on Computational Linguistics (Coling 2014) held in Dublin, Ireland. The conference is organized by the Centre for Global Intelligent Content (CNGL) and held at the Helix Conference Centre at Dublin City University (DCU) from 25–29 August 2014, under the auspices of the International Committee on Computational Linguistics (ICCL).

COLING is almost 50 years old, its first gathering having taken place in New York in 1965. It has been organized once every two years, initially in odd years and then in even years, after COLING 1976 in Ottawa. Throughout its long history, COLING's aspiration to provide an amicable forum for participants with broad backgrounds to present and share their ideas remains the same. We believe that the inherent complexity of language is worthy of study from diverse perspectives and that COLING provides a venue for fruitful interdisciplinary interaction.

We accepted 217 papers (138 oral presentations and 79 poster presentations) from 685 effective submissions, having received 705 submissions in total. Regardless of the format of presentation, all of the accepted papers were allocated 12 pages in the proceedings.

The review process of a large conference such as COLING is always complex and occasionally encounters difficulties. The program committee has to cope with the challenges of selecting which papers to accept among a large quantity of high quality submissions. The task of choosing 217 papers from 685 strong submissions covering the ever broadening fields of computational linguistics was not an easy one.

To cope with the anticipated difficulties, we asked six senior colleagues to join the Scientific Advisory Board (SAB) and help us through all stages of reviewing papers. They are: Ralph Grishman (New York University, USA), Yuji Matsumoto (NAIST, Japan), Joakim Nivre (Uppsala Univ., Sweden), Michael Picheny (IBM TJ Watson Research Center, USA), Donia Scott (Univ. of Sussex, UK), and Chengqing Zong (CAS, China).

We had 20 thematic areas and each area was chaired by two or more area chairs. Thanks to over 800 responsive reviewers, the review process proceeded in a very smooth manner, and each paper was read at least by three reviewers. In some cases, papers and their reviews were carefully assessed by Area Co-Chairs, one of the SAB members and by us, in our roles as Program Committee Co-Chairs. We are extremely happy with the very strong set of papers that has been accepted for presentation at the conference. It is, however, with regret that we had no choice but to reject a large number of high quality papers, due to the sheer volume of submissions received.

We would like to thank the SAB members and the Program Committee Area Chairs for their dedicated and efficient review work, and our reviewers for their professionalism in delivering high quality reviews. We also thank the authors of all the papers for submitting their fruits of labour to COLING. Although we were only able to accept a small subset of the submitted papers, we do hope that all authors and reviewers have benefited from this process of indirect dialogue.

Last but not least, we would like to thank the people who made COLING 2014 and this volume possible. We thank General Chairs, Josef van Genabith (Universität des Saarlandes/DFKI) and Andy Way (CNGL, DCU), and the chairs of the Local Organizing Committee, Cara Green (CNGL, DCU) and John Judge (CNGL/NCLT, DCU), for their tireless work. We are especially grateful to the Publications Chairs, Joachim Wagner (CNGL, DCU), Liadh Kelly (CNGL, DCU) and Lorraine Goeuriot (CNGL, DCU), for their hard work in preparing the proceedings.

Prof. Jan Hajic (Charles University, Czech Republic)
Prof. Junichi Tsujii (Microsoft Research, China)
COLING 2014 Program Committee Co-Chairs
July 8, 2014

Welcome from the General Chairs

We are very pleased indeed to welcome you all to COLING 2014, the 25th International Conference on Computational Linguistics. We are particularly proud that the ICCL selected Dublin City University (DCU) as the location of COLING 2014.

DCU and its National Centre for Language Technology (NCLT) have a long track record in NLP. Unlike India, the previous COLING host country, Ireland is a very small country. A unique feature of the Irish University landscape is that universities team up with industry partners and each other to pool expertise to form large research centres. DCU is a founding member of CNGL, the Centre for Gobal Intelligent Content. COLING 2014 is organised by DCU in partnership with the CNGL, and as General Chairs we are proud to represent both DCU and CNGL.

The conference is taking place at the Helix Conference Centre, a stunning building added to the DCU campus in 2002. DCU is a young, dynamic and ambitious university; since admitting its first students in 1980, DCU has grown in both student numbers and size and now occupies a 72-acre site in Glasnevin, just to the north of Dublin city centre. To date almost 50,000 students have graduated from DCU and are now playing significant roles in enterprise and business globally. Today in 2014, DCU delivers more than 200 programmes to over 12,000 students across its four faculties — Humanities and Social Sciences, Science and Health, Engineering and Computing and DCU Business School. DCU's excellence is recognised internationally and it is ranked among the top-50 young Universities worldwide (QS 'Top 50 under 50' 2013). In the last eight years, DCU has twice been named Sunday Times 'University of the Year'.

At the time of writing, the total number of people registered to attend COLING has exceeded 675. With delegates from 58 countries, COLING 2014 will witness a colourful diversity of language and culture, which is appropriate given that Dublin is known as the localisation capital of the world. Some evidence for this comes from our sponsors, to whom we are extremely grateful: Baidu, eBay, Microsoft, Symantec and Google.

We are very pleased with the programme that has been assembled for you, comprising of four days for the main conference with a total of 138 oral presentations, 79 posters and a special track with 28 demo presentations, two days of workshops and tutorials before the main conference, and other satellite workshops immediately after. 18 topical workshops with a sharp focus on issues of key interest today will be attended by about 191 delegates, and the 6 high-quality tutorials are sure to attract large crowds. Social events include a welcome reception on the evening of 24th August, the conference banquet in the Guinness Storehouse on 26th, and excursions to some beautiful places of interest on 27th.

When DCU was awarded COLING two years ago, our own personal situations were quite different. One of us was away working in the translation industry in the UK, while the other was leading the Science Foundation Ireland and Industry-funded CNGL research center. Over the past few months, we have changed countries, and jobs: Andy is back as Deputy Director of the CNGL's Centre for Intelligent Content, while Josef has moved to Saarbrücken to take up a Chair and a Scientific Directorship at DFKI.

While these changes were taking place, we both had the backing of a remarkable team. The organization of an event on the scale of COLING takes enormous energy, planning and commitment from a large number of individuals. We have assembled a large, competent team of volunteers who are available to assist you while you are here in Dublin. We are sure that all of you participating at COLING — at tutorials, workshops, or the main conference — will enjoy the time you spend here in Ireland, and will look back on the event as one of the most memorable that you attend. Finally, thanks to all of you for coming. We hope you all enjoy the conference, that you benefit from the excellent programme that has been assembled, and that you go away from here having made new friends.

Prof. Josef Van Genabith (Universität des Saarlandes/DFKI, Germany)
Prof. Andy Way (CNGL, DCU, Ireland)

Organisers

General Chairs
Prof. Andy Way, CNGL, Dublin City University, Ireland
Prof. Josef van Genabith, Universität des Saarlandes/DFKI, Germany

Programme Chairs
Prof. Junichi Tsujii, Microsoft Research, China
Prof. Jan Hajic, Charles University, Czech Republic

Workshops Chairs
Dr. Jennifer Foster, CNGL, Dublin City University, Ireland
Prof. Dan Gildea, University of Rochester, USA
Prof. Tim Baldwin, University of Melbourne, Australia

Publication Chairs
Dr. Joachim Wagner, CNGL, Dublin City University, Ireland
Dr. Liadh Kelly, CNGL, Dublin City University, Ireland
Dr. Lorraine Goeuriot, CNGL, Dublin City University, Ireland

Publicity Chairs
Dr. Dorothy Kenny, SALIS, Dublin City University, Ireland
Prof. Seong-Bae Park, Kyungpook National University, Korea

Local Chairs
Dr. Cara Greene, CNGL, Dublin City University, Ireland
Dr. John Judge, CNGL / NCLT, Dublin City University, Ireland

Scientific Advisory Board
Prof. Joakim Nivre, Uppsala Univ., Sweden
Prof. Yuji Matsumoto, NAIST, Japan
Dr. Michael Picheny, IBM TJ Watson Research Center, USA
Prof. Donia Scott, Univ. of Sussex, UK
Prof. Chengqing Zong, CAS, China
Prof. Ralph Grishman, New York University, USA

Tutorial Chairs
Prof. Qun Liu, CNGL, Dublin City University, Ireland
Prof. Fei Xia, University of Washington, USA

Demo Chairs
Dr. Lamia Tounsi, CNGL, Dublin City University, Ireland
Dr. Rafal Rak, NaCTeM, University of Manchester, UK

Sponsorship Chairs
Dr. Páraic Sheridan, CNGL, Dublin City University, Ireland
Prof. Hans Uszkoreit, DFKI, Germany
Dr. Huaping Zhang, Beijing Institute of Technology, China
Dr. Hiromi Nakaiwa, NTT, Japan

Table of Contents

Conference Program

Saturday, 23rd of August 2014

Biomedical/Clinical NLP
Ozlem Uzuner, Meliha Yetisgen and Amber Stubbs

Using Neural Networks for Modeling and Representing Natural Languages
Tomas Mikolov

Sunday, 24th of August 2014

Multilingual Word Sense Disambiguation and Entity Linking
Roberto Navigli and Andrea Moro

Automated Grammatical Error Correction for Language Learners
Joel Tetreault and Claudia Leacock

Selection Bias, Label Bias, and Bias in Ground Truth
Anders Søgaard, Barbara Plank and Dirk Hovy

Dependency Parsing: Past, Present, and Future
Wenliang Chen, Zhenghua Li and Min Zhang

Biomedical/clinical NLP

Ozlem Uzuner
Information Studies
University of Albany, SUNY
Albany, NY
ouzuner@albany.edu

Meliha Yetişgen
Biomedical and
Health Informatics
University of Washington
Seattle, WA
melihay@uw.edu

Amber Stubbs
Library and
Information Science
Simmons College
Boston, MA
stubbs@simmons.edu

Introduction

Recent years have seen a rapid growth in the use of biomedical documents and narrative clinical records for applications outside of direct patient care. Accordingly, recent years have also seen an increase in the development of NLP technologies for concept and relation extraction, summarization, and question answering on these data.

This tutorial will present an overview of the biomedical and clinical NLP data, tools, and methods with the intent of providing the researchers with a jump-start into these domains. We will focus on the demand for NLP in biomedical and clinical domains, the potential for impact, and the required NLP tasks. We will introduce this information in the following categories:

Overview of biomedical/clinical NLP

Biomedical narratives are often dense with domain-specific jargon. Clinical narratives, in addition to being dense with domain-specific jargon, exhibit the complexities of a specialized sub-language. They are written by the domain experts and for the domain experts. Their primary purpose is to assist in informing future decisions about the care of the patients. As a result, both biomedical and clinical narratives present challenges for existing open-domain NLP technologies and require special considerations for their accurate understanding and interpretation.

In this section, we will discuss the data sources currently available to researchers, as well as provide an overview of the research questions both domains. On the clinical side, this includes using EHRs for phenotyping and decision support systems. The biomedical side uses NLP to explore fields such as literature-based discovery and literature searches.

Current research questions in biomedical and clinical NLP

NLP applications are generally built to answer specific questions about data. In this section, we will provide examples of the types of questions researchers are asking in the clinical and biomedical domains. Additionally, we will discuss how different linguistic aspects of these data are addressed by looking at existing syntactic (part of speech tagging, parsing) and semantic (concept extraction, temporal information extraction, coreference resolution) systems.

Datasets and the annotation process

Building annotated corpora for any task can be challenging, but the biomedical and clinical domains have additional barriers that make creating these corpora difficult. In this section, we will discuss available annotated resources in both domains, and discuss challenges in biomedical and clinical corpus building, such as restrictions on data access and the need for domain experts to be part of the annotation process.

Clinical Annotation Case Study

The 2014 i2b2 NLP Shared Task[1] involved two NLP challenges: 1) de-identification of medical records, and 2) identification of risk factors for coronary artery disease in diabetic patients. Each of these tracks required a separate annotation effort, and in this portion of the tutorial we will describe the end-to-end process of creating this annotated resource, from data selection to writing the annotation guidelines to creating the final gold standards.

NLP Methods

Just as there are many research questions in the biomedical and clinical domains, there are many existing NLP systems that address these questions. In this portion of the tutorial, we will describe the three main approaches (rule-based, statistical, and hybrid) commonly used to process biomedical and clinical text. Additionally, we will present on-going research projects from our research labs including (1) extracting structure and semantics from clinical text through section segmentation and assertion analysis and (2) clinical applications such as phenotype modeling and specific examples of information extraction in the radiology domain.

Open questions and future directions

Research in the fields of biomedical and clinical NLP is far from complete; the end of this tutorial will look at current unsolved problems in these fields, as well as look ahead towards potential future research questions.

Acknowledgements

This tutorial was supported in part by Informatics for Integrating Biology and the Bedside (i2b2) award No. 2U54LM008748 from the National Institutes of Health (NIH)/National Q5 Library of Medicine (NLM), by award No. 1R13LM01141101 from the NIH NLM, by award No. 1R21EB016872 from NIH NIBIB, and by Institute of Translational Health Sciences award No. UL1TR000423 from NIH NCATS.

[1] `https://www.i2b2.org/NLP/HeartDisease/`

Using Neural Networks for Modeling and Representing Natural Languages

Tomas Mikolov
Facebook A.I. Research
One Hacker Way, Menlo Park
California, US
tmikolov@fb.com

Artificial neural networks are powerful statistical models that have been shown to provide excellent results in a number of domains. In the last few years, the computer vision and automatic speech recognition communities have been heavily influenced by these techniques. Applications to problems that involve natural language, such as machine translation or computational semantics, are becoming mainstream in the NLP research.

This tutorial aims to introduce the basic concepts and provide intuitive understanding of neural networks, including the very popular field of deep learning. This should help the researchers who are entering this field to quickly understand the major tricks of the trade.

The structure of the tutorial is as follows:

Basic machine learning applied to natural language

- n-grams and bag-of-words representations
- logistic regression, support vector machines

Introduction to neural networks

- architecture of neural networks: neurons, layers, synapses
- activation function
- objective function
- training: stochastic gradient descent, backpropagation, learning rate, regularization
- multiple hidden layers and intuitive explanation of deep learning

Distributed representations of words

- basic application of neural networks for obtaining vector representation of words
- linguistic regularities in the word vector space
- word analogy tasks with vector representations
- representations of phrases and sentences
- simple application to machine translation of words and phrases

Neural network based language models

- feedforward and recurrent neural net architectures for language modeling
- class based softmax, hierarchical softmax
- joint training with maximum entropy model
- recurrent model with slow features
- application to language modeling, speech recognition, machine translation

Tips for future research

- understanding the current research culture
- hints how to recognize good papers and ideas
- promising future directions

Resources

- introduction to open-source software: RNNLM toolkit, word2vec and other tools
- links to large text corpora, pre-trained models
- benchmark datasets for advancing the state of the art

Multilingual Word Sense Disambiguation and Entity Linking

Roberto Navigli and **Andrea Moro**
Dipartimento di Informatica, Sapienza Università di Roma
Viale Regina Elena 295, 00161 Roma, Italy
{moro, navigli}@di.uniroma1.it

Tutorial Motivation and Description

Nowadays the textual information available online is provided in an increasingly wide range of languages. This language explosion clearly forces researchers to focus on the challenging problem of being able to analyze and understand text written in any language. At the core of this problem lies the lexical ambiguity of language, an issue which is addressed by two key tasks in computational lexical semantics: multilingual Word Sense Disambiguation (WSD) and Entity Linking (EL).

WSD (Navigli, 2009) is a historical task in Computational Linguistics aimed at explicitly assigning meanings to word occurrences within text, while EL (Erbs et al., 2011; Rao et al., 2013; Cornolti et al., 2013) is a recent task focused on finding mentions of entities within a text and linking them to the most suitable entry in a knowledge base, if one exists. The two main differences between WSD and EL are in the kind of inventory used, i.e. dictionary vs. encyclopedia, and the assumption that the mention is complete or potentially incomplete, respectively. Notwithstanding these differences, the tasks are pretty similar in nature, in that they both involve the disambiguation of textual fragments in a given language according to a reference inventory. Nevertheless, the research community has tackled the two tasks separately, often duplicating efforts and solutions. Moreover, the vast majority of the state-of-the-art approaches only marginally take into account languages different from English.

In this tutorial, we present the two tasks of multilingual WSD and EL, by surveying the challenges involved and the most effective solutions, both in isolation by illustrating the state of the art in the two fields, and when the tasks are addressed in a unified, multilingual way.

In particular, this tutorial covers three key aspects of the multilingual WSD and EL tasks:

1. Multilingual inventories of word senses and named entities;

2. State-of-the-art methods to perform disambiguation and linking;

3. Evaluation of the systems: gold standard datasets and performance measures.

The tutorial is aimed at stressing the key challenges of the tasks of WSD and EL when moving from a monolingual to a multilingual setup. The tutorial includes examples and discussions intended to illustrate and clarify the major challenges of the tasks and which solutions are most appropriate to which problem.

Organization of the tutorial

The half-day tutorial contains sessions on the following topics:

1. Introduction (30 mins) This first session will provide the necessary background, definitions and examples for the two considered tasks: multilingual WSD and EL.

2. The multilingual inventory for word senses and named entities (45 mins) In this session we will overview the definitions of the inventories used in state-of-the-art approaches both for WSD and

EL. We will then discuss the key aspects of partial matching for EL and, finally, we will describe multilingual inventories of word senses and named entities, among which Open Multilingual WordNet (Bond and Foster, 2013), Wikipedia[1], DBpedia (Auer et al., 2007), BabelNet (Navigli and Ponzetto, 2012).

3. State of the art in WSD and EL (75 mins) This session will introduce the key challenges to the tasks of WSD and EL and the well-known approaches, such as IMS (Zhong and Ng, 2010) and UKB (Agirre et al., 2013) for WSD, and Babelfy (Moro et al., 2014), AIDA (Hoffart et al., 2011; Hoffart et al., 2012), Tagme (Ferragina and Scaiella, 2010; Ferragina and Scaiella, 2012), Illinois Wikifier (Cheng and Roth, 2013) and DBpedia Spotlight (Mendes et al., 2011; Daiber et al., 2013), that can partially address them. Challenges include: the lack of training data for non-English languages, the granularity of the sense inventory, the high level of ambiguity in EL, the most frequent sense baseline challenge, etc.

4. Evaluation measures and gold standard datasets (30 mins) We will conclude the tutorial by describing the standard performance measures for these tasks and well-known datasets for multilingual WSD and EL together with a discussion of the results.

Speakers

Roberto Navigli is an associate professor in the Department of Computer Science at the Sapienza University of Rome. He is the recipient of an ERC Starting Grant in computer science and informatics on multilingual word sense disambiguation (2011-2016) and a co-PI of a Google Focused Research Award on Natural Language Understanding. His research interests lie in the field of Word Sense Disambiguation and Induction, multilingual knowledge acquisition and applications of lexical semantics.
Andrea Moro is a PhD student in the Department of Computer Science at the Sapienza University of Rome. His research interests focus on Natural Language Understanding with an emphasis on Unsupervised Relation Extraction, Word Sense Disambiguation and Entity Linking.

Acknowledgments

erc The authors gratefully acknowledge the support of the ERC Starting Grant MultiJEDI No. 259234.

References

Eneko Agirre, Oier Lopez de Lacalle, and Aitor Soroa. 2013. Random Walks for Knowledge-Based Word Sense Disambiguation. *Computational Linguistics*.

Sören Auer, Christian Bizer, Georgi Kobilarov, Jens Lehmann, Richard Cyganiak, and Zachary Ives. 2007. DBpedia: A Nucleus for a Web of Open Data. In *Proc. of ISWC/ASWC*, pages 722–735.

Francis Bond and Ryan Foster. 2013. Linking and extending an open multilingual wordnet. In *Proc. of ACL*, pages 1352–1362.

Xiao Cheng and Dan Roth. 2013. Relational Inference for Wikification. In *Proc. of EMNLP*.

Marco Cornolti, Paolo Ferragina, and Massimiliano Ciaramita. 2013. A framework for benchmarking entity-annotation systems. In *Proc. of WWW*, pages 249–260.

Joachim Daiber, Max Jakob, Chris Hokamp, and Pablo N. Mendes. 2013. Improving Efficiency and Accuracy in Multilingual Entity Extraction. In *Proc. of I-Semantics*.

Nicolai Erbs, Torsten Zesch, and Iryna Gurevych. 2011. Link Discovery: A Comprehensive Analysis. In *Proc. of ICSC*, pages 83–86.

[1] http://wikipedia.org

Paolo Ferragina and Ugo Scaiella. 2010. TAGME: on-the-fly annotation of short text fragments (by wikipedia entities). In *Proc. of CIKM*, pages 1625–1628.

Paolo Ferragina and Ugo Scaiella. 2012. Fast and accurate annotation of short texts with wikipedia pages. *Software, IEEE*, 29(1):70–75, Jan.

Johannes Hoffart, Mohamed Amir Yosef, Ilaria Bordino, Hagen Fürstenau, Manfred Pinkal, Marc Spaniol, Bilyana Taneva, Stefan Thater, and Gerhard Weikum. 2011. Robust Disambiguation of Named Entities in Text. In *Proc. of EMNLP*, pages 782–792.

Johannes Hoffart, Stephan Seufert, Dat Ba Nguyen, Martin Theobald, and Gerhard Weikum. 2012. KORE: keyphrase overlap relatedness for entity disambiguation. In *Proc. of CIKM*, pages 545–554.

Pablo N. Mendes, Max Jakob, Andrés García-Silva, and Christian Bizer. 2011. DBpedia spotlight: shedding light on the web of documents. In *Proc. of I-Semantics*, pages 1–8.

Andrea Moro, Alessandro Raganato, and Roberto Navigli. 2014. Entity Linking meets Word Sense Disambiguation: A Unified Approach. *Transactions of the Association for Computational Linguistics*.

Roberto Navigli and Simone Paolo Ponzetto. 2012. BabelNet: The automatic construction, evaluation and application of a wide-coverage multilingual semantic network. *Artificial Intelligence*, 193:217–250.

Roberto Navigli. 2009. Word sense disambiguation: A survey. *ACM Comput. Surv.*, 41(2):1–69.

Delip Rao, Paul McNamee, and Mark Dredze. 2013. Entity linking: Finding extracted entities in a knowledge base. In *Multi-source, Multilingual Information Extraction and Summarization*, pages 93–115. Springer.

Zhi Zhong and Hwee Tou Ng. 2010. It Makes Sense: A Wide-Coverage Word Sense Disambiguation System for Free Text. In *Proc. of the ACL 2010 System Demonstrations*, pages 78–83, Uppsala, Sweden, July. Association for Computational Linguistics.

Automated Grammatical Error Correction for Language Learners

Joel Tetreault
Yahoo Labs
111 W. 40th Street
New York, NY, 10018, USA
tetreaul@yahoo-inc.com

Claudia Leacock
McGraw-Hill Education CTB
22 Ryan Ranch Road
Monterey, CA, 93940
claudia.leacock@ctb.com

Tutorial Description

A fast growing area in Natural Language Processing is the use of automated tools for identifying and correcting grammatical errors made by language learners. This growth, in part, has been fueled by the needs of a large number of people in the world who are learning and using a second or foreign language. For example, it is estimated that there are currently over one billion people who are non-native writers of English. These numbers drive the demand for accurate tools that can help learners to write and speak proficiently in another language. Such demand also makes this an exciting time for those in the NLP community who are developing automated methods for grammatical error correction (GEC). Our motivation for the COLING tutorial is to make others more aware of this field and its particular set of challenges. For these reasons, we believe that the tutorial will potentially benefit a broad range of conference attendees.

In general, there has been a surge in interest in using NLP to address educational needs, which in turn, has spawned the recurring ACL/NAACL workshop "Innovative Use of Natural Language Processing for Building Educational Applications" that had its 9th edition at ACL 2014. The last three years, in particular, have been pivotal for GEC. Papers on the topic have become more commonplace at main conferences such as ACL, NAACL and EMNLP, as well as two editions of a Morgan Claypool Synthesis Series book on the topic (Leacock et al., 2010; Leacock et al., 2014). In 2011 and 2012, the first shared tasks in GEC (Dale and Kilgarriff, 2011; Dale et al., 2012) were created, and dozens of teams from all over the world participated. This was followed by two successful CoNLL Shared Tasks on the topic in 2013 and 2014 (Ng et al., 2013; Ng et al., 2014).

While there have been many exciting developments in GEC over the last few years, there is still considerable room for improvement as state-of-the-art performance in detecting and correcting several important error types is still inadequate for real world applications. We hope to engage researchers from other NLP fields to develop novel and effective approaches to these problems. Our tutorial is specifically designed to:

- Introduce an NLP audience to the challenges that language learners face and thus the challenges of designing NLP tools to assist in language acquisition
- Provide a history of GEC and the state-of-the-art approaches for different error types
- Show the need for multi-lingual error correction approaches and discuss novel methods for achieving this
- Discuss ways in which error correction techniques can have an impact on other NLP tasks

Outline

1. Introduction
2. Special Problems of Language Learners
    - Errors made by English Language Learners (ELLs)
    - Influence of L1
3. Heuristic and Data Driven Approaches to Error Correction
    (a) Early heuristic rule-based methods
    (b) Methods for detection and correction
    (c) Types of training data
    (d) Features
    (e) Web-based methods
4. Annotation and Evaluation
    (a) Annotation schemes
    (b) Proposals for efficient annotation
    (c) Evaluation Measures
    (d) Crowdsourcing for annotation and evaluation
5. Current Trends in Error Correction
    (a) Detection of ungrammatical sentences and Other error types
    (b) Shared tasks
    (c) Going beyond the classification methodology
    (d) Error correction in other languages
6. Conclusions

Organizers

Joel Tetreault is a Senior Research Scientist at Yahoo Labs in New York City. His research focus is Natural Language Processing with specific interests in anaphora, dialogue and discourse processing, machine learning, and applying these techniques to the analysis of English language learning and automated essay scoring. Previously he was Principal Manager of the Core Natural Language group at Nuance Communications, Inc. where he worked on the research and development of NLP tools and components for the next generation of intelligent dialogue systems. Prior to Nuance, he worked at Educational Testing Service for six years as a Managing Senior Research Scientist where he researched automated methods for detecting grammatical errors by non-native speakers, plagiarism detection, and content scoring. Tetreault received his B.A. in Computer Science from Harvard University (1998) and his M.S. and Ph.D. in Computer Science from the University of Rochester (2004). He was also a postdoctoral research scientist at the University of Pittsburgh's Learning Research and Development Center (2004-2007), where he worked on developing spoken dialogue tutoring systems. In addition he has co-organized the Building Educational Application workshop series for 7 years, the CoNLL 2013 Shared Task on Grammatical Error Correction, and is currently NAACL Treasurer.

Claudia Leacock is a Research Scientist at McGraw-Hill Education CTB who has been working on using NLP in educational applications for 20 years focusing on automated scoring and grammatical error detection. She was previously a consultant for Microsoft Research where she collaborated on the development of ESL Assistant: a web-based prototype tool for detecting and correcting grammatical errors of English language learners. As a Distinguished Member of Technical Staff at Pearson Knowledge

Technologies, and previously as a Principal Development Scientist at Educational Testing Service, she developed tools for automated assessment of short-response content-based questions and for grammatical error detection. As a member of the WordNet group at Princeton University's Cognitive Science Lab, her research focused on word sense disambiguation. Dr. Leacock received a B.A. in English from NYU, a Ph.D. in Linguistics from the City University of New York, Graduate Center and was a post-doctoral fellow at IBM, T.J. Watson Research Center.

References

Robert Dale and Adam Kilgarriff. 2011. Helping Our Own: The HOO 2011 pilot shared task. In *Proceedings of the Generation Challenges Session at the 13th European Workshop on Natural Language Generation*, pages 242–249, Nancy, France, September. Association for Computational Linguistics.

Robert Dale, Ilya Anisimoff, and George Narroway. 2012. HOO 2012: A report on the preposition and determiner error correction shared task. In *Proceedings of the Seventh Workshop on Building Educational Applications Using NLP*, pages 54–62, Montréal, Canada, June. Association for Computational Linguistics.

Claudia Leacock, Martin Chodorow, Michael Gamon, and Joel Tetreaukt. 2010. *Automated grammatical error detection for language learners.* Morgan & Claypool Publishers.

Claudia Leacock, Martin Chodorow, Michael Gamon, and Joel Tetreaukt. 2014. *Automated grammatical error detection for language learners, second edition.* Morgan & Claypool Publishers.

Hwee Tou Ng, Siew Mei Wu, Yuanbin Wu, and Joel Tetreault. 2013. The conll-2013 shared task on grammatical error correction. In *Proceedings of the Seventeenth Conference on Computational Natural Language Learning*, Sofia, Bulgaria, August. Association for Computational Linguistics.

Hwee Tou Ng, Siew Mei Wu, Ted Briscoe, Christian Hadiwinoto, Raymond Hendy Susanto, and Christopher Bryant. 2014. The conll-2014 shared task on grammatical error correction. In *Proceedings of the Eighteenth Conference on Computational Natural Language Learning: Shared Task*, pages 1–14, Baltimore, Maryland, June. Association for Computational Linguistics.

Selection Bias, Label Bias, and Bias in Ground Truth

Anders Søgaard, Barbara Plank, and Dirk Hovy
Center for Language Technology
University of Copenhagen
soegaard@hum.ku.dk, {bplank|dhovy}@cst.dk

Introduction

Language technology is biased toward English newswire. In POS tagging, we get 97–98 words right out of a 100 in English newswire, but results drop to about 8 out of 10 when running the same technology on Twitter data. In dependency parsing, we are able to identify the syntactic head of 9 out of 10 words in English newswire, but only 6–7 out of 10 in tweets. Replace references to Twitter with references to a low-resource language of your choice, and the above sentence is still likely to hold true.

The reason for this bias is obviously that mainstream language technology is data-driven, based on supervised statistical learning techniques, and annotated data resources are widely available for English newswire. The situation that arises when applying off-the-shelf language technology, induced from annotated newswire corpora, to something like Twitter, is a bit like when trying to predict elections from Xbox surveys (Wang et al., 2013). Our induced models suffer from a data *selection bias*.

This is actually not the only way our data is biased. The available resources for English newswire are the result of human annotators following specific guidelines. Humans err, leading to *label bias*, but more importantly, annotation guidelines typically make debatable linguistic choices. Linguistics is not an exact science, and we call the influence of annotation guidelines *bias in ground truth*.

In the tutorial, we present various case studies for each kind of bias, and show several methods that can be used to deal with bias. This results in improved performance of NLP systems.

Selection Bias

The situation that arises when applying off-the-shelf language technology, induced from annotated newswire corpora, to something like Twitter, is, as mentioned, a bit like when trying to predict elections from Xbox surveys. In the case of elections, however, we can correct most of the selection bias by post-stratification or instance weighting (Wang et al., 2013). In language technology, the bias correction problem is harder.

In the case of elections, you have a single output variable and various demographic observed variables. All values taken by discrete variables at test time can be assumed to have been observed, and all values observed at training time can be assumed to be seen at test time. In language technology, we typically have several features only seen in training data and several features only seen in test data.

The latter observation has led to interest in bridging unseen words to known ones (Blitzer et al., 2006; Turian et al., 2010), while the former has led to the development of learning algorithms that prevent feature swamping (Sutton et al., 2006), i.e., that very predictive features prevents weights associated with less predictive, correlated features from being updated. Note, however, that post-stratification (Smith, 1988) may prevent feature swamping, and that predictive approaches to bias correction (Royall, 1988) may solve both problems. Instance weighting (Shimodaira, 2000), which is a generalization of post-stratificiation, has received some interest in language technology (Jiang and Zhai, 2007; Foster et al., 2011), but most work on domain adaptation in language technology has focused on predictive approaches, i.e., semi-supervised learning (Reichart and Rappoport, 2007; Sagae and Tsujii, 2007; McClosky et al., 2010; Chen et al., 2011).

Selection bias introduces a bias in $P(X)$. Note that, in theory, this should not hurt discriminative algorithms trying to estimate $P(Y|X)$, without estimating $P(X)$, but in practice it still does. The inductive bias of our algorithms and the size our samples make our models sensitive to selection bias (Zadrozny, 2004). Predictive approaches try to correct this bias by adding more (pseudo-labeled) data to the training sample, while post-stratification and instance weighting reweigh the data to make $P(X)$ similar to the distribution observed in the population. As mentioned, this will never solve the problem with unseen features, since you cannot up-weigh a null feature.

Semi-supervised learning can correct modest selection bias, but if the domain gap is too wide, our initial predictions in the target domain will be poor, and semi-supervised learning is likely to increase bias rather than decrease it. However, recent work has shown that semi-supervised learning can be combined with distant supervision and correct bias in cases where semi-supervised learning algorithms typically fail (Plank et al., 2014).

In the tutorial we illustrate these different approaches to selection bias correction, with discriminative learning of POS taggers for English Twitter as our running example.

Label Bias

In most annotation projects, there is an initial stage, where the project managers compare annotators' performance, compute agreement scores, select reliable annotators, adjudicate, and elaborate on annotation guidelines, if necessary. Such procedures are considered necessary to correct for the individual biases of the annotators (*label bias*). However, this is typically only for the first batches of data, and it is well-known that even some of the most widely used annotated corpora (such as the Penn Treebank) contain many errors (Dickinson and Meurers, 2003) in the form of inconsistent annotations of the same n-grams.

Obviously, using non-expert annotators, e.g., through crowd-sourcing platforms, increase the label bias considerably. One way to reduce this bias involves collecting several annotations for each datapoint and averaging over them, which is often feasible because of the low cost of non-expert annotation. This is called majority voting and is analogous to using ensembles of models to obtain more robust systems.

In the tutorial we discuss alternatives to averaging over annotators, incl., using EM to estimate annotator confidence (Hovy et al., 2013), and joint learning of annotator competence and model parameters (Raykar and Yu, 2012).

Bias in Ground Truth

In annotation projects, we use inter-annotator agreement measures and annotation guidelines to ensure consistent annotations. However, annotation guidelines often make linguistically debatable and even somewhat arbitrary decisions, and inter-annotator agreement is often less than perfect. Some annotators, for example, may annotate *social*in *social media* as a noun, others may annotate it as an adjective. In this part of the tutorial, we discuss how to correct for the bias introduced by annotation guidelines. For both label bias and bias in ground truth, we, again, use POS tagging for English Twitter as our running example.

Evaluation

Once we accept our data is biased in different ways, we need to reconsider model evaluation. If our data was selected in a biased way, say from a few editions of the Wall Street Journal, does significance over data points make much sense? If our annotators have individual biases, can we no longer evaluate our models on the data of one or two annotators? If the annotation guidelines introduce biases in ground truth, can we somehow correct for that? In practice we typically do not have hundreds of datasets annotated by different annotators using different annotation guidelines, but in the tutorial we present various ways of, nevertheless, correcting for some of these biases.

Acknowledgements

This research is funded by the ERC Starting Grant LOWLANDS No. 313695.

References

John Blitzer, Ryan McDonald, and Fernando Pereira. 2006. Domain adaptation with structural correspondence learning. In *EMNLP*.

Minmin Chen, Killiang Weinberger, and John Blitzer. 2011. Co-training for domain adaptation. In *NIPS*.

Markus Dickinson and Detmar Meurers. 2003. Detecting errors in part-of-speech annotation. In *EACL*.

Jennifer Foster, Ozlem Cetinoglu, Joachim Wagner, Josef Le Roux, Joakim Nivre, Deirde Hogan, and Josef van Genabith. 2011. From news to comments: Resources and benchmarks for parsing the language of Web 2.0. In *IJCNLP*.

Dirk Hovy, Taylor Berg-Kirkpatrick, Ashish Vaswani, and Eduard Hovy. 2013. Learning whom to trust with MACE. In *NAACL*.

Jing Jiang and ChengXiang Zhai. 2007. Instance weighting for domain adaptation in NLP. In *ACL*.

David McClosky, Eugene Charniak, and Mark Johnson. 2010. Automatic domain adaptation for parsing. In *NAACL-HLT*.

Barbara Plank, Dirk Hovy, Ryan McDonald, and Anders Søgaard. 2014. Adapting taggers to Twitter with not-so-distant supervision. In *COLING*.

Vikas C. Raykar and Shipeng Yu. 2012. Eliminating Spammers and Ranking Annotators for Crowdsourced Labeling Tasks. *Journal of Machine Learning Research*, 13:491–518.

Roi Reichart and Ari Rappoport. 2007. Self-training for enhancement and domain adaptation of statistical parsers trained on small datasets. In *ACL*.

R Royall. 1988. The prediction approach to sampling theory. In Rao Krishnaiah, editor, *Handbook of Statistics*. North-Holland.

Kenji Sagae and Jun'ichi Tsujii. 2007. Dependency parsing and domain adaptation with LR models and parser ensembles. In *EMNLP-CoNLL*.

Hidetoshi Shimodaira. 2000. Improving predictive inference under covariate shift by weighting the log-likelihood function. *Journal of Statistical Planning and Inference*, 90:227–244.

T Smith. 1988. Post-stratification. *The Statistician*, 40.

Charles Sutton, Michael Sindelar, and Andrew McCallum. 2006. Reducing weight undertraining in structured discriminative learning. In *NAACL*.

Joseph Turian, Lev Ratinov, and Yoshua Bengio. 2010. Word representations: a simple and general method for semi-supervised learning. In *ACL*.

Wei Wang, David Rotschild, Sharad Goel, and Andrew Gelman. 2013. Forecasting elections with non-representative polls. *Forthcoming in International Journal of Forecasting*.

Bianca Zadrozny. 2004. Learning and evaluating classifiers under sample selection bias. In *ICML*.

Dependency Parsing: Past, Present, and Future

Wenliang Chen and Zhenghua Li and Min Zhang
School of Computer Science and Technology,
Soochow University, China
{wlchen, Zhli13, mzhang}@suda.edu.cn

Dependency parsing has gained more and more interest in natural language processing in recent years due to its simplicity and general applicability for diverse languages. The international conference of computational natural language learning (CoNLL) has organized shared tasks on multilingual dependency parsing successively from 2006 to 2009, which leads to extensive progress on dependency parsing in both theoretical and practical perspectives. Meanwhile, dependency parsing has been successfully applied to machine translation, question answering, text mining, etc.

To date, research on dependency parsing mainly focuses on data-driven supervised approaches and results show that the supervised models can achieve reasonable performance on in-domain texts for a variety of languages when manually labeled data is provided. However, relatively less effort is devoted to parsing out-domain texts and resource-poor languages, and few successful techniques are bought up for such scenario. This tutorial will cover all these research topics of dependency parsing and is composed of four major parts. Especially, we will survey the present progress of semi-supervised dependency parsing, web data parsing, and multilingual text parsing, and show some directions for future work.

In the first part, we will introduce the fundamentals and supervised approaches for dependency parsing. The fundamentals include examples of dependency trees, annotated treebanks, evaluation metrics, and comparisons with other syntactic formulations like constituent parsing. Then we will introduce a few mainstream supervised approaches, i.e., transition-based, graph-based, easy-first, constituent-based dependency parsing. These approaches study dependency parsing from different perspectives, and achieve comparable and state-of-the-art performance for a wide range of languages. Then we will move to the hybrid models that combine the advantages of the above approaches. We will also introduce recent work on efficient parsing techniques, joint lexical analysis and dependency parsing, multiple treebank exploitation, etc.

In the second part, we will survey the work on semi-supervised dependency parsing techniques. Such work aims to explore unlabeled data so that the parser can achieve higher performance. This tutorial will present several successful techniques that utilize information from different levels: whole tree level, partial tree level, and lexical level. We will discuss the advantages and limitations of these existing techniques.

In the third part, we will survey the work on dependency parsing techniques for domain adaptation and web data. To advance research on out-domain parsing, researchers have organized two shared tasks, i.e., the CoNLL 2007 shared task and the shared task of syntactic analysis of non-canonical languages (SANCL 2012). Both two shared tasks attracted many participants. These participants tried different techniques to adapt the parser trained on WSJ texts to out-domain texts with the help of large-scale unlabeled data. Especially, we will present a brief survey on text normalization, which is proven to be very useful for parsing web data.

In the fourth part, we will introduce the recent work on exploiting multilingual texts for dependency parsing, which falls into two lines of research. The first line is to improve supervised dependency parser with multilingual texts. The intuition behind is that ambiguities in the target language may be unambiguous in the source language. The other line is multilingual transfer learning which aims to project the syntactic knowledge from the source language to the target language.

In the fifth part, we will conclude our talk by discussing some new directions for future work.

Outline

- Part A: Dependency parsing and supervised approaches
  - A.1 Introduction to dependency parsing
  - A.2 Supervised methods
  - A.3 Non-projective dependency parsing
  - A.4 Probabilistic and generative models for dependency parsing
  - A.5 Other work
- Part B: Semi-supervised dependency parsing
  - B.1 Lexical level
  - B.2 Partial tree level
  - B.3 Whole tree level
  - B.4 Other work
- Part C: Parsing the web and domain adaptation
  - C.1 CoNLL 2007 shared task (domain adaptation subtask)
  - C.2 Works on domain adaptation
  - C.3 SANCL 2012 (parsing the web)
  - C.4 Text normalization
  - C.5 Attempts and challenges for parsing the web
- Part D: Multilingual dependency parsing
  - D.1 Dependency parsing on bilingual text
  - D.2 Multilingual transfer learning for resource-poor languages
  - D.3 Other work
- Part E: Conclusion and open problems

Instructors

Wenliang Chen received his Bachelor degree in Mechanical Engineering and Ph.D. degree in computer science from Northeastern University (Shenyang, China) in 1999 and 2005, respectively. He joined Soochow University since 2013 and is currently a professor in the university. Prior to joining Soochow University, he was a research scientist in the Institute for Infocomm Research of Singapore from 2011 to 2013. From 2005 to 2010, he worked as an expert researcher in NICT, Japan. His current research interests include parsing, machine translation, and machine learning. He is currently working on a syntactic parsing project where he applies semi-supervised learning techniques to explore the information from large-scale data to improve Dependency parsing. Based on the semi-supervised techniques, he developed a dependency parser, named DuDuPlus (http://code.google.com/p/duduplus/), for the research and industry communities.

Zhenghua Li is currently an assistant professor in Soochow University. He received his PhD in Computer Science and Technology from Harbin Institute of Technology (HIT) in April 2013. Zhenghuas research interests include natural language processing and machine learning. More specifically, his PhD research focuses on the dependency parsing of the Chinese language using discriminative machine-learning approaches. He has been working on joint POS tagging and dependency parsing (EMNLP 2011, COLING 2012), and multiple treebank exploitation for dependency parsing (ACL 2012).

Min Zhang, a distinguished professor and Director of the Research Center of Human Language Technology at Soochow University (China), received his Bachelor degree and Ph.D. degree in computer science from Harbin Institute of Technology in 1991 and 1997, respectively. From 1997 to 1999, he worked as a postdoctoral research fellow in Korean Advanced Institute of Science and Technology in South Korea. He began his academic and industrial career as a researcher at Lernout & Hauspie Asia Pacific (Singapore) in Sep. 1999. He joined Infotalk Technology (Singapore) as a researcher in 2001 and became a senior research manager in 2002. He joined the Institute for Infocomm Research (Singapore) as a research scientist in Dec. 2003. His current research interests include machine translation, natural language processing, information extraction, social network computing and Internet intelligence. He has co-authored more than 150 papers in leading journals and conferences, and co-edited 10 books/proceedings published by Springer and IEEE. He was the recipient of several awards in China and oversea. He is the vice president of COLIPS (2011-2013), the elected vice chair of SIGHAN/ACL (2014-2015), a steering committee member of PACLIC (2011-now), an executive member of AFNLP (2013-2014) and a member of ACL (since 2006). He supervises Ph.D students at National University of Singapore, Harbin Institute of Technology and Soochow University.

Author Index

Association for Computational Linguistics
209 N. Eighth Street
Stroudsburg, Pennsylvania 18360

proceedings.com

52nd Annual Meeting of the Association for Computational Linguistics (ACL 2014)

Tutorial Abstracts

Baltimore, Maryland, USA
22 June 2014

ISBN: 978-1-63439-194-8